JAMES BOND 007
COLLECTION

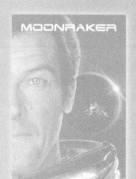

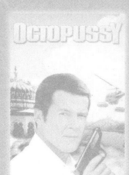

This instrumental series is arranged for Flute, Trumpet, Clarinet, Alto Sax, Tenor Sax and Trombone.
The arrangements are completely compatible with each other and can be played together or as solos.
In addition, an optional piano accompaniment book is also available.

Project Manager: CAROL CUELLAR
Music Editor: BILL GALLIFORD
Art Layout: MICHAEL RAMSAY
Arranged by BILL GALLIFORD, ETHAN NEUBURG and DAVID PUGH
Recordings by ARTEMIS MUSIC LIMITED

CONTENTS

007 THEME
(From "From Russia With Love")

Music by JOHN BARRY

THE JAMES BOND THEME

(From "Dr. No")

Music by MONTY NORMAN

IFM0037CD

DIAMONDS ARE FOREVER
(From "Diamonds Are Forever")

Lyric by DON BLACK
Music by JOHN BARRY

IFM0037CD

LIVE AND LET DIE
(From "Live and Let Die")

Words and Music by
PAUL McCARTNEY and
LINDA McCARTNEY

Live and Let Die - 2 - 1
IFM0037CD

FOR YOUR EYES ONLY
(From "For Your Eyes Only")

Lyrics by MICHAEL LEESON
Music by BILL CONTI

FROM RUSSIA WITH LOVE
(From "From Russia With Love")

Words and Music by
LIONEL BART

GOLDEN EYE
(From "Golden Eye")

Words and Music by
BONO and THE EDGE

IFM0037CD

GOLDFINGER
(From "Goldfinger")

Lyrics by LESLIE BRICUSSE
and ANTHONY NEWLEY
Music by JOHN BARRY

IFM0037CD

THE MAN WITH THE GOLDEN GUN
(From "The Man With the Golden Gun")

Lyric by DON BLACK
Music by JOHN BARRY

IFM0037CD

BARON SAMEDI'S DANCE OF DEATH
(From "Live and Let Die")

Music by GEORGE MARTIN

MOONRAKER
(From "Moonraker")

Lyric by HAL DAVID
Music by JOHN BARRY

ALL TIME HIGH
(From "Octopussy")

Lyric by TIM RICE
Music by JOHN BARRY

IFM0037CD

DO YOU KNOW HOW CHRISTMAS TREES ARE GROWN?

(From "On Her Majesty's Secret Service")

Lyric by HAL DAVID
Music by JOHN BARRY

IFM0037CD

ON HER MAJESTY'S SECRET SERVICE

(From "On Her Majesty's Secret Service")

Music by JOHN BARRY

WE HAVE ALL THE TIME IN THE WORLD
(From "On Her Majesty's Secret Service")

Lyric by HAL DAVID
Music by JOHN BARRY

NOBODY DOES IT BETTER
(From "The Spy Who Loved Me")

Lyrics by CAROLE BAYER SAGER
Music by MARVIN HAMLISCH

MISTER KISS KISS BANG BANG

(From "Thunderball")

Lyric by LESLIE BRICUSSE
Music by JOHN BARRY

IFM0037CD

YOU ONLY LIVE TWICE
(From "You Only Live Twice")

Lyric by LESLIE BRICUSSE
Music by JOHN BARRY

THUNDERBALL
(From "Thunderball")

Lyric by DON BLACK
Music by JOHN BARRY

TOMORROW NEVER DIES
(From "Tomorrow Never Dies")

Words and Music by
SHERYL CROW and
MITCHELL FROOM

A VIEW TO A KILL
(From "A View to a Kill")

Words and Music by
DURAN DURAN and JOHN BARRY

IFM0037CD

SURRENDER
(From "Tomorrow Never Dies")

Words and Music by
DAVID ARNOLD, DON BLACK
and DAVID McCALMONT

LICENCE TO KILL
(From "Licence to Kill")

Words and Music by
ANTHONY NEWLEY, JEFFERY COHEN,
LESLIE BRICUSSE, NARADA MICHAEL WALDEN,
WALTER AFANASIEFF and JOHN BARRY

THE LIVING DAYLIGHTS
(From "The Living Daylights")

Words and Music by
JOHN BARRY and PAL WAAKTAAR

The Living Daylights - 2 - 1
IFM0037CD

THE WORLD IS NOT ENOUGH
(From "The World Is Not Enough")

Lyrics by DON BLACK
Music by DAVID ARNOLD